Muddy I

Selected P(

SERGEY STRATANOVSKY was born in 1944 in Leningrad and educated in the department of Russian philology at Leningrad University. He began to write poetry in 1968, around the time of the Prague Spring and his graduation, though his early work subsisted in a culture of Soviet Union censorship. During this period Stratanovsky was part of Russia's underground literary culture, and he co-edited the *samizdat* magazines *Dialog* and *Obvodny Kanal (Bypass Canal)*. With the relaxation of censorship following the Perestroika reforms in the 1980s Stratanovsky's work gained a wider public readership. Since 1993 he has authored twelve collections of poems, and his work has been translated into Bulgarian, Chechen, Dutch, English, Estonian, Finnish, French, Hebrew, Italian, German, Lithuanian, Polish, and Swedish. In 2000 he was awarded the inaugural Joseph Brodsky Memorial Fellowship.

J. KATES is a poet, literary translator and the president and co-director of Zephyr Press, a non-profit press that focuses on contemporary works in translation from Russia, Eastern Europe and Asia. A former president of the American Literary Translators Association, he is the recipient of multiple awards including the Cliff Becker Book Prize in Translation. He has published three chapbooks of his own poems: *Mappemonde* (Oyster River Press), *Metes and Bounds* (Accents Publishing) and *The Old Testament* (Cold Hub Press), as well as a full book, *The Briar Patch* (Hobblebush Books). He is the translation editor of *Contemporary Russian Poetry* and the editor of *In the Grip of Strange Thoughts: Russian Poetry in a New Era*. His works of translation include titles by Tatiana Shcherbina, Mikhail Aizenberg, Jean-Pierre Rosnay, Mikhail Yeryomin, Regina Derieva, Aleksey Porvin, Nikolai Baitov, and Genrikh Sapgir.

SERGEY STRATANOVSKY

MUDDY RIVER

Selected Poems

translated by J. Kates

CARCANET

First published in Great Britain in 2016
by Carcanet Press Limited
Alliance House, 30 Cross Street
Manchester, M2 7AQ
www.carcanet.co.uk

A CIP catalogue record for this book is available from the
British Library: ISBN 9781847772534

The publisher acknowledges financial assistance from
Arts Council England.

Contents

Introduction

Russian poets who dominated the first half of the twentieth century did so not only on the strength of their creative work, but also as literary and personal witnesses to an age. For the most part, the poets who were born into the second half of the twentieth century and came of cultural age then and at the beginning of the twenty-first disclaimed this monumental role, and have chosen a more individual expression – under the circumstances, itself a kind of political choice and declaration, but with a different import. A few poets, however, have remained at least overtly conscious in their work of the continuing dislocations and evolutions of their times, often with a lighter touch than their predecessors. Among these, Sergey Stratanovsky stands out.

Sergey Georgevich Stratanovsky was born in 1944 into an academic family, his father a classicist who had translated the histories of Herodotus and Thucydides into Russian, and his mother a university professor of French who also practiced translation. Stratanovsky began writing young, and in high school made the acquaintance of a fellow poet and lifelong friend, Viktor Krivulin. He studied Philology at the University of Leningrad in the mid-1960s, in the literary company of Krivulin, Elena Shvarts and Elena Ignatova. During his student years, however, he made no claim to writing poetry, but graduated from the Leningrad University with a degree in history, and then worked as a guide and a librarian.

Stratanovsky dates the beginning of his writing poems to 1968, a year he identifies with the 'Prague Spring' and his graduation from university – characteristically, one political and one personal event. He took part in a short-lived Literary Association of the Union of Writers, led by the poet Gleb Semenov, whom he, like many others, thought of as his real teacher. Among the members of this literary association were Krivulin and Ignatova, Boris Kupriyanov, Victor Shirali, and others associated with poetry in Leningrad. In the 1970s, he began publishing in unofficial literary circles, and served as the editor, with Kyrill Butyrin, of the *samizdat* magazine *Obvodny Canal*. He began having his poems published outside the Soviet Union in 1977, but his first full book did not come out – in Russia – until 2003, after a period of literary silence in the 1990s. Stratanovsky was the first winner of the Brodsky Fellowship for residence in Italy. He was awarded the Andrey Bely Prize in 2010 and the Giosie Carducci in 2011. As of now, he has seen eight separate collections of his poetry appear in Russia, and this, his third in translation, is his first in English.

Stratanovsky's poetry has changed over the years, but always with a strong sociological eye and a deeply religious soul. 'I draw a sharp line between the ideas of verse and poetry,' Stratanovsky has written, 'believing that poetry is an aesthetic concept rather than a genre. Since 1968, my work has evolved considerably. In the late 1970s I moved from traditional rhyme to a mixed verse in which less formal lines replaced rhyme. In the 1990s a principle of the poetic fragment, in a style resembling Rozanov's, but in verse, dominated. Thematically, my work is rather diverse: As much as I have written pure poetry, so also have I written on historical, social and theological topics. At one time or another different themes were uppermost: In the early 90s, for instance, social themes dominated my poetry.'

More recently, Stratanovsky's verse has reflected his responses to the myths and folklore of the peoples of Russia and beyond. 'Pkharmat Unbound', which dramatises a Chechen version of the classic myth of Prometheus defying ultimate power, resonates with formal reference to antiquity, Russian literary tradition (think of The Grand Inquisitor) and contemporary geopolitics. Its very subtitle, characterising it as a 'действо', a specific kind of antiquated Christian liturgical play, witnesses the complexity of reference. (Calling it a 'mystery play' is a ham-handed approximation.) Boundaries of space and time blur. Politics, culture, and theology interpenetrate. 'Pkharmat Unbound' ends with a deceptively simple affirmation, as does the parallel dialogue, 'Job and the Arab'. Is this key poem a meditative *midrash*, or is it a contemporary reflection on 1990s Russia?

A more ambiguous conclusion marks the short story in prose, 'The Mountain Sary-Tau'. This narrative drawn from a Tatar epic begins under the mountain Sary-Tau in present-day Kazakhstan, within the Golden Horde at the end of the fourteenth century, and it touches on both Mongol and Islamic tradition before moving into the world of Slavonic monasticism. The move is far from straightforward, though, as the ending demonstrates. The words are simple, the implications unfathomable.

A disingenuous naïveté bringing to mind a school of 'primitivism' may be the defining oxymoron of Stratanovsky's diction, sophistication disguised as innocence. Although Stratanovsky is often included in the Leningrad trio with Krivulin and Shvarts, Nikita Eliseev made a key distinction in citing him for the Andrey Bely Prize in 2010: 'Alongside the complicated surrealism of Elena Shvarts and Victor Krivulin [Stratanovsky's poetry] is marked by its apparent simplicity. If we speak of pictorial equivalents of poetry, the poetry of Stratanovsky is reminiscent of the paintings of Pirosmani or Henri Rousseau. He does not paint in half-tones. The clash of clear, bright colours and sharp lines – this is his poetry.'

This sets up a constant tension in Stratanovsky's work between external environments – physical, political, sociological – and internal landscapes. What mediates between these are the religions of his culture, or the cultures of his religion. Outer life is defined in the clear, bright colours and sharp lines; the inner life in pastels and the murkiness of a muddy river. But these qualities are not separable. As the poet and critic Mikhail Aizenberg has expressed it, 'The poems of Stratanovsky give us a picture (established in words) of a consciousness where these realities do not exist in isolation from each other, not in different, cultured cells separated by partitions. In his poems there is a single world, the different parts of which meaningfully reflect and explain each other.

'There is a proposition that true innovation is inseparable from some archaising intentions, and this proposition is confirmed by the verses of Stratanovsky. It is very difficult in a few words to point to an unprecedented quality in his work.

It seems to me that his particularity is not even in *how* it is expressed, but *from where* it is articulated, there where sound has its source. From somewhere terribly deep: in a time of faith and magic, where and when element and consciousness are not divided and continue to constitute a meaningful whole.'

*

I was first introduced to Sergey Stratanovsky in 1986 in the apartment of our mutual friends Grigory Benevich and Olga Popova, whose interest in poetry is framed by their immersion in theology and religious studies. I am grateful to them for the introduction, as well as to the poet himself, who has encouraged and corrected me in equal measure for three decades now. The earliest poems in this book were handed to me in blurred typescript on flimsy onionskin, *samizdat*. The most recent ones have come electronically straight from the poet's own machine, or plucked off the Internet. It is a fairly common practice among Russian poets to date their poems more or less precisely. Stratanovsky has done this irregularly; and, for the most part, I have followed a rough chronological placement here, but not strictly so, especially as the poet has reprinted some poems in subsequent collections. Where he himself has printed the poems with dates, I have included these. In the present setting, Stratanovsky's untitled poems begin part-way down the page and are referred to by their first line.

Translating Stratanovsky is an adventure in historical, mythological, and ecclesiastical research. The work has led me to the canals of St Petersburg, the steppes of Central Asia, the mountains of the Caucasus, and the landscape of Palestine. As a translator, perhaps the single greatest liberty I've taken with the Russian texts has been with the poem that gives a title to this collection. The original adjective непрозрачный goes into English most literally as 'not-transparent'. Obviously, the closest English word has to be 'opaque', but this conveys nothing of the noun it goes with. Rivers are not opaque. 'Unclear', while catching the litotes, has a semantic range too wide for the Russian. A further interpretation, perhaps the most accurate, is 'murky'.

I chose 'muddy' instead partly to avoid the engine-revving-like sound of 'murky river' but also as a kind of in-joke: the town in which many of these translations were written, edited and compiled was named Muddy River at its incorporation (two years after the founding of St Petersburg) and the officially-named Muddy River still runs through it, as murky waters, from the Obvodny ('Bypass') Canal and the Chernaya Rechka (Black Stream) to the grand Nevà itself, flow through Stratanovsky's poems. A long way from these, another clouded watercourse stands also for the act of translation itself, which gains energy from local currents and wordwide elements. In making these translations, I have been grateful for the help not only of the poet himself, but also for the expertise of Amy Adams, Grigory Benevich and Olga Popova, Peter France, Olga Partan, and Ra'ad Siraj. I hope this collection repays and honors them all.

MUDDY RIVER

Selected Poems

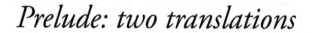

Prelude: two translations

Смерть не таинственный порог
Она привычна как творог
Она печётся как пирог
На каждый день и час.

И по ночам когда не спишь
Она скребётся словно мышь
И льдинкой бьётся в нас.

Death is no doorstep into mysteries.
It is a cake rising in the oven.
It is as commonplace as cottage cheese,
a daily, hourly companion.

There are nights when sleep comes hard.
death creeps in like a little mouse
and needles us with a shard of ice.

Ленинградская лестница,
щи,
коммунальная дверь,
Провода от звонков:
Иванов, Розенцвейг, Иванов,
В шапке снега бескровного,
с холода,
зябкими пальцами спичку –
В коммунальную бестолочь, выморочь,
в джунгли обид в коридоре.
Там женщина плачет в смятенье и горе,
В норе бытия
без любви и без света.
И ни единым словом не согрета.

A Leningrad stairwell
>cabbage soup,
>a communal doorway,

Doorbell wires:
>Ivanov, Rosenzweig, Ivanov,

In a hat of anaemic snow,
>from the cold,
>with chilly fingers a match –

Into the communal muddle, exhaustion,
>into that jungle of grievances the corridor.

There a woman weeps in confusion and sorrow,
In the burrow of her existence
>without love and without light.

Unwarmed by a single word.

FROM

POEMS

Стихи

1993

In a white bedroom it is quiet, quiet
From the white ceiling
My sorrowing shoulderless
Little brother looks down.

He hangs there, holding a hammer
A mouthful of nails
You dropped by a little too soon
My sweet little brother.

Through the small window a white light
Illuminates him now
Wait, dear heart
                    wait a little bit
All of a half hour more.

· 1968–1972 ·

Outside on the streets in summer light
Drinking water and apple juice
Aimlessly loafing, aimlessly
Letting go, not even trying to hear
How somewhere an untied sack
destined for death is breathing
How a child goes on terrifying
Wretched, good-for-nothing fathers
So the season frightens you half awake
Through your pain and you hide your face
On the streets of a castaway summer
Excursions, children's games
And pain from the animal light
Of love and death to come

· 1970 ·

Nail like a dreadful boy in the corner
Is calling with a quiet finger.
But like ice on the Nevà River
yesterday's day stirred in the brain.

Only the future is a shining ray
We're living only for the future
But in the corner the children play
With Nail, their quiet little brother.

· 1973 ·

The Obvodny Canal

Look, over there are the mute and sullen souls
Of Cannery and Bakery.
And there is an industrial sky
In the canal.
And pain is all the more deliberate and deaf,
And in the beginning
There was this pain...
Factory smoke streams past in the canal,
An autumn day just glimmering, glimmering,
And the letters of the Saltworks sign
Walk on water.
And it seems: I am absolutely not I.
Among the factories, warehouses
hospitals and gaunt faces
I have become silence and the rubbish of living.

·1969·

Herostratos and Herostratos

And we are all
Herostratos son of Herostratos,
Disseminators
                    of a world-wide fire,
Arsonists of treasuries of raw material
And storehouses of the harvest.
See how we strike our matches
On a fall night, out in the rain –
We the destroyers of things,
Seeking a terrible ecstasy.
But out there living on the edge of life
A vegestability up against heaven
Beyond the Black Stream, a vegetable bin
Like fat-rumped Aphrodite
hopped up on her own tomatoes.
We lay on our beds dreaming of her
And here she is, as a matter of fact,
And the grove where Pushkin fought
Shines in her vicinity,
And here the Black Stream flows
Even blacker than any Grecian Styx –
Happy the one who drank from its current,
He did not, and will not die.
Not for him, but for us
Flows the terrible water of oblivion.
On a fall night, out in the rain,
We will abandon this wretched life
For an unknown destination.
Run from that terror of oblivion,
Run, as Evgeny once

Fled the Bronze Horseman in a trashed land.
Wherever in slush and mist
Urinous warehouses stand,
An empty harvest for the city stores,
Like all-embracing ecstasy,
waits for the Herostratic brand.
We are a sudden squall, a menace,
We are quiet thieves like mice.
And like the fiery rose
You will ignite, and perish.
Well then,
                we are all
Herostratos son of Herostratos,
Wastrels of the Promethean fire,
Arsonists of treasuries of raw material
And storehouses of the harvest.

· 1970–71 ·

Sociological Tract in Verse on the Phenomenon of Alcoholism

By some miracle you and I
escape the emptiness of life!

And sorrow, like a stale bagel
burning in an alcoholic mouth.
A human being creeps in the alley,
treated by everyone like swine.
But once upon a time,
his photos showed
a proud, handsome worker.
He lived, rejoicing in the achievements
of his own collective.
He had a home, a family
and sons in school
studying dialectic,

                              but lost
the essence of life,
and discovered in alcohol
oblivion and himself.
O, phenomenon of alienation,
Sisyphean life, useless labour!
Houses alive like hallucinations,
the flow of muddy canals.
O Leningrad, a land empty
and unkind to your people –
here demons from China
stir up the slow waters in the canals.
Here the utilities of Lenergy:
Lenlight, Lengas, Lenbrain,

suck like hungry vampires
and you bow under them,
a trivial human bridge
between birth and the grave.
Past canals and houses
through an awkward, harsh light
and years in an unhappy world
even a bird flies over the bay
as if in prison,
ignorant of freedom.
China will gobble it up
after disasters and calamities.
No one ever offered it
the Promised Land.
And a human being with a heavy head
creeps along the sidewalk,
brooding and watchful
treated by everyone like swine
like society's ulcer
and life's own rubbish.

· 1971 ·

Street Games

Right now it's a council of war
              at the home of the Great Wolf Vitalik
Slavka has come with his tomahawk
              Grishka with his father's knife
The army of Red Wolves
              prepares for tomorrow's mix-up
With the army of the Gray Ravens
              from the alley of Raisa the Thief
Slingshots are ready for battle, sticks and dead rats
Tomorrow the fences and stairwells
              will be spattered with blood
We don't need to give way
              to the rotten eggs of ravens
Tomorrow in the street fight
              we will be victorious, repeating
The name of the Great Wolf

· 1978 ·

The Hermitage

1

Yes, I've been to the Hermitage. Everything there
Is store-bought. Fleshy dames gaze lewdly from the walls,
Here a Roman bosom propositions Papa, while elsewhere
Mothers weep for Christ taken down from the cross.

This is foreign to us and wafts nothing of our grief
To that coming world as plain as a blue balloon,
Cherubs, goddesses, Jews not to be imagined alive –
They only cripple the mind, but do not heal our pain.

2

Burn Raphael, who stole into the Hermitage like a thief
The flame will run like a sooty tiger from floor to floor
Burn Raphael, what good to you are the eyes of the Virgin
If you yourself, Emelia, have been cheated by fate from birth.

3

On the Destruction of 'Danae'

Before the dark soul,
        Before the spite of Lithuanian bogs
She is defenceless
        And pays full measure for the offences
Of her alien tribe,
        And Eros grimaces from weeping
Knows it must be –
        her beauty without force
Before a boor's revenge.

· 1981–83 ·

The Terrorist

'A death slap
           to the angel of a greasy paradise,
to twittering sex-parks,
           and a string of seductions,
to gaping porno-burrows,
           to church-services, to the tickling of God,
to their common weal, incorruptible heaven,
their democracies, parties, television sets and seaside villas
A death-slap, abomination, abomination... vengeance.'

They're hunting for the killer: Who can he be? Arab? Italian?
German? Mongol? The computer spits out possibilities
Who is he, this citizen of destruction?
                     A real person – or a ghost
From a work of a century ago
                     in sodden, febrile Petersburg
A confection from underground
                     a phantom out of the mind of Dostoevsky

· 1988 ·

Fantasia on Psalm 1

Shaking the bosom of land and sea
The wind will raise a noxious chaff –
You are chaff, apostates from the Law,
Bodies that burn even as they revel

Only that man is blessed who shuns
The sinful houses of the wicked
Their tongues are black and flattering
Their dainties tainted like a sickness

They will not prostrate themselves
Before God at their dreadful feasts
Their sinews might as well be wolves
Fox-hearts beating in their breasts.

Cupped in the hands of God you are
But empty clay, the stuff of Earth.
Intent on God, fixed in the Law
Lives the blessèd man of worth.

Blind to the brutality of judges
Deaf to his own worst enemies
By the waters of a loud and worldly mob,
By that river stands, just like a tree.

· 1972 ·

Bible Notes

1

Receptacles of grief and joy
        Abraham His Puppet
Moses His Puppet
        prophets, rulers in Zion
And in His immense hand
The Temple seems a pebble
Receptacles of wrath and trembling
        of wars, of holocausts and kingdoms
Thou shalt not know His Name
        thou shalt not find His footstep
He enters flesh like a knife
He steals life like a thief

· 1978 ·

2

See Him make Nothing from density –
        An insubstantial flame
A storm in the Wilderness of Zion
A storm on the waters –
        overwhelming the human vessel
See Him the guide and leader
        through the body of the iron bull
Like an illness
        His eyes blazed
The ancient image –
        Thunder over his stiffnecked people

· 1982 ·

3
Isaac v. Abraham

God or one of his angels
Happening to fly past
      restrained his hand then
I neither know nor want to know
I can't imagine to whom
These quarrels might now be of interest
But all the same I'll tell the story.
Having awakened in the morning,
I stepped outside the tent and saw:
Two of our slaves,
      two young men, bought for us
At the market in Salem,
      wielding Chaldean axes
For a burnt offering
Nearby my father Abraham
bent over a whetstone
As dark as a stormcloud
      whetting his sacrificial knife –
'Is there a festival today,'
      I asked Abraham –
'Why hast thou commanded
the firewood, father, and why
Art thou whetting your knife?
      Does the Lord ask once again
For some exceptional sacrifice?'
My father answered nothing,
But ordered the slaves to lay on my shoulders
The bundle of wood
      and the two of us walked the road
To the land of Moriah
Three days and three nights,

and finally in front of us
Appeared the foothills of the mountains
          and again I asked Abraham,
'Where is the lamb, father,
          for the burnt offering?'
And again my father did not answer
Only then,
          when we took the path into the mountain
And laid the wood in order,
          only then I looked
Abraham in the eyes
          and saw the eyes of a man
Become a tiger
With a hunter's leap
          he jumped me. I fell
On the logs face downward
          knocked out by the blow
And saw when I woke up
          how the sacrificial ropes bound me
From my knees to my shoulders
Either an angel happening
to fly past restrained his hand
From outright evildoing
          or the terrible Lord decided not
          to feast on my flesh
I neither know nor want to know
'My long-awaited boy,'
          my father babbled among his tears,
'My son Isaac,
          thou art saved from the teeth of the Lord
and henceforth our nation
          will shine in the deserts of the ages
For my obedience,
          for my going where God sends me

And according to His word
        that region where we wander now
Will become our land.'
I did not answer.
I kept silent, all along the slippery path
Sloping back into the valley.

· 1990 ·

4

I don't know who it was
        They didn't tell me his name
Was He Someone similar
        to me, my father or brother
Or did Someone incorporeal
        Walk the earth in that time?
I was young then.
        In Mizraim, in the sweaty land
we were construction slaves
        my brothers and father
the servants of Pharaoh, overseers
        spitefully mocked us
We hated them
I remember the sacred night
        We stayed awake in our quarters,
The moon like a sacrificial knife
        quietly gleamed over the earth
I remember how we ate the lamb
        burning our fingers, choking on excitement
And then, leaning over,
my father said, Listen,
        over our barracks,
          listen how

The Lord passes over the land
           smiting the people of Mizraim
Slaying the firstborn of every house
           with a butcher knife
Only a child then, I don't remember
           what happened next
I remember camping, tents
           somewhere in the desert
Livestock that died of hunger,
           the grumbling of the exhausted, the embittered
'Who is He?' –
           I asked then –
           'Why did He lead us away?
What does He need from us?'

· 1982 ·

5

I am the watchman on the wall
           of the Jericho stronghold
on the horizon, far off
           I see the enemy camp
I see the innumerable host
           of the merciless nomads of God
I know that, spying out our land,
           they were here in the city,
I know that the dirty whore Rahab
           entertained them
I know: these walls will fall
           before the armies of their God
I know that I will be spitted
           at noon in the holy slaughter

· 1982 ·

6

In the year of our aggression
        We exterminated with our swords
the inhabitants of this land
        given to us as our heritage
by our Lord...
We consumed their grapes...
        drank up the water from their wells
Black was the aspect of the land,
        but its living gods remained,
And here now, in the night,
they move among us
        the tongueless, dispossessed gods
moving among us and watching
        fiercely watching

· 1982 ·

7

In fear the enemies returned
        with golden propitiating gifts
A holy box – a shrine (an ark)
        generator of immense wrath
Excitedly the people rejoiced
        with tears the Levites prayed
We beggars ran
        around the settlement with ecstatic cries
'God has returned home from captivity
        to our village'
We ran with the joyful news
        and suddenly began to argue haphazardly
As inside the little box

He dwelled, the Almighty,
holding the sea and the land
        unbounded like the sky above us
We quarrelled and decided
        to steal to the ark
to open its lid, and look
        at the dwelling of the Living God
It's not that I overslept then
        I simply lost my courage, didn't leave my home
Like a mouse I trembled in my bed,
        kept quiet from fear, and in the morning
People found at the ark
        crowds of teenagers laid low
By the hand that chastises the world.

· 1983 ·

8

And so we came back home
        from our long eastern captivity
We are the descendants of Jacob
        God's chosen people
We wept when we saw
        the destruction of our dwellings
our gardens turned into wasteland
        and the Temple of Solomon in wreckage
There was a man among us
        who called himself wise
a Leader of the nation, keeper
        of the letters and of the holy stories
Angrily he reproached us
        with falling away from the ancient ways
He called for the redemption of sins

he recruited for the urgent building
of a new House of the Lord
I remember I was one of the first
        to inscribe myself willingly
I worked like a slave for a year,
        and then a prophet –
a programmer of the people's happiness
        was promoted to overseer for his zeal
I remember that morning
        the suppliers brought on their carts
trunks of Cedars of Lebanon
        to buttress the holy walls
We hauled them up with straps
        until one broke and the cedar
Collapsed, maiming me
Since when I am a cripple
        a beggar under the walls of the temple
Rearing heavenwards
        to the Lord of all our prayers
I beg for my daily bread
        and try in vain to understand
By what sin then did I earn
        this injury from the All-High
How had I failed to satisfy Him?

· 1983 ·

9

'God will strike with a thunderbolt
        all those who piss in their beds.'
Thus spoke our instructor
        the worthy schoolmaster
of the temple school

And happy little boys –
        lion cubs of the Law of Sinai
Smeared me with filth
        for my night-time indecencies
Beat me, spat in my face
        and chortled:
'You pervert, you
        Moabite's son, half-breed'
Oh, how I bleated then
        how I prayed Almighty God
To take my life
        give me a quiet death
I wept bitterly then
        And a consoler appeared to me
An iron Angel from Heaven.
'Boy,' he said, 'neither weep nor grumble,
        nor nurse your grievances
God will reward you
        for your unchildlike sorrow
You will be a great prophet,
        a teller of the life to come
You will be glorified like an emperor
        among the stiffnecked descendants
Of Abraham, my servant.
        So, for now, swallow
           insult with your daily soup
Bear pain and beatings
        Nothing comes cheap
Your grief is not for your sins,
        but for your future gift.'

· 1984 ·

A Letter to My Brother

My brother, my beloved brother
            I am in freedom, you in a dungeon
Tomorrow you will be executed
            as a witness to the Crucifixion
Lord, our Saviour

Brother, my brother,
            You hold me in contempt, I know
Before the image of Cæsar
            I bowed as if to God
I softened with a sacrifice
            his unbaptised clay
Yes, I bent my soul
            pro forma, as a ritual
For everybody knows
            that Cæsar is not God

Brother, my brother,
            I showed my frailty, yes but listen
Does not each one of us, like you, strive
            for Heavenly Truth according to our strength?
Each bearing our own torment?
            Is it really true the Lord sculpted
Our flesh for martyrdom?

My brother, brother mine,
            You will bear your crimson halo
Into the province of the resurrected,
            while I, rejected, vanish
It is painful and bitter to me, brother,
            even yesterday my speechless grief
Drew me to the mountains
            to perish like a wounded bird
In solitude

Long I wandered in the mountains
       and in my grieving loneliness remembered
How to our city not long ago
       a crafty preacher came,
the learnèd Alexandriets.
       With withering scorn he spoke
About martyrs to their faith!
       'Idiots!' he reiterated, 'asses
Imitating Christ,
       while Christ Himself suffered not at all
In his Ghostly body
       He climbed the tree of torment
Untouched by mortal pain'

I remember, how you, trembling,
       cried out, 'Away, you foreigner,
Heretic errant servant of Satan, begone
Of all our false-tongued abusive men
       you are worse than the heathen,

There is no place for you among us'
Silenced, shrugging his shoulders,
       the preacher left for home
With fury all of us Christians
       condemned his crooked speech
But then just yesterday, in my
       mortal grief
       along the trail above a beckoning precipice
Suddenly I thought:
       what if the foreigner was right
Our Saviour did not suffer
       and our whole faith in error?

· 1984 ·

A Trip to Visit My Brother in the Psychiatric Hospital

It was madness, it was madness, it was
the meaningless look on my brother's face
        right through me, through the thick of the hospital
A look through the thick, through and through
        piercing the walls, into the uninhabited Nothing
A chink... a nail in the intellect...
        brittle reason banging noises
(Somewhere at his wordforge a blacksmith
        like nails is forging these sounds:
A chink... through... and through and through)

It was speechless... bleached lightning... it was...
Lightning piercing right through
        the layer of white custom
Cutting through
        world-wide copies with keen understanding

Nowadays can you remember
        The Lord's Easter, my sweet brother?
The Resurrection of Christ
        you remember that, do you remember
How we used to go in the early morning
        to the teeming church, and afterwards
off to visit our religious friends,
        we sat around the holiday table
Eating the sanctified Easter cakes,
        Do you really not remember, think hard
He doesn't answer... he has forgotten.

Savage... an empty halfbeast
        in striped hospital clothing
What's left for us to do

and, God, why have you brought down
Your power to bear on him?

'He believed too intensely,' said
            the unbelieving psychiatrist,
'He prayed too obsessively
            in the churches for hours on end
He took communion, he fasted,
            sang in the choir, to what end?
God did not help him,
            but you are the guilty one, no god,
You overlooked the psychosis
            falsely calling it inspiration
A maelstrom from on high
            and behold the effect of delusion.

'But maybe he is contented,' said
            the assistant on the ward,
'Contented in an unhealthy world
            this world of ours
He has no need to stake a claim to.'

They led the patient away
            My time with him was over
I left the hospital
            a foul wind blew across Russia
Somewhere a drunken nation
            began to howl out a ribald song

In these times who remembers
            The Lord's Easter today?
Do I really have to give this scavenger
            who climbed into the trolleybus
the Kiss of Peace, is this drunken bum one with me?

An inclement wind moaned
        on that day when the sons of God
came to present themselves before the Lord
        and the Adversary came also among them
And the Adversary said:
        I know Thy servant
The contented Herdsman,
        doth he fear God for naught?
Test him, Lord,
        strike down his herd with pestilence
Smash his ribs
        smite his skin with sore boils
Only do not touch his intellect,
        For the One Who Holds the World needs reason
To argue with a madman.

And this man, who has now become, thanks
To sour wine and bread-and-tears, this man,
Who has become a living wild animal
In an alien life. Was he really the one
Who used to walk with us beside the quiet waters
Barefoot over pebbles and instructed the people
Who spoke obscurely, who stumbled over words
Sideways with trouble, trouble, like a nincompoop
Making choices – Is he really now the bread
Of God, a pathway to the Tree of Paradise,
And a small boat bobbing on the sea of life?

· 1982 ·

FROM

DARK DAY

Тъма Дневная

2000

Look at Pavka Chichikov,
   yesterday a Party hack,
 Today the master of a firm
    selling the most Russian naked souls
      to lemon-scented Singapore.

You hear what a racket they make
      at the Uranium Heaven Café
The R & D bureaucrat
      and the apocapolitico.
Eating and drinking together
      as they hatch out their pickled plans
For global catastrophe.

The day of the fall of Troy
                    the fury of the ancient massacre
When the stones were shrieking,
                    sprayed with the sticky, hot
bioliquids of corpses

The day of the fall of Troy...
                    But the blood will not be obliterated
The act of the crime will become
                    an airy design on vases
Wall paintings and mosaics
                    the song of a blind man at a feast
Singing of spearcarrying heroes

The Veteran's Tale

An episode from the war memoirs of Boris Slutsky.

It was a pity, of course...
        wartime, and Russia
White snow, a starry track
        on the Smolensk road, on any road at all...

Well, this Fritz was a good guy,
        a cut-up, guttural muttering.
He muttered something there,
        played his harmonica, sang a little
and danced as best he could.

We laughed, we fed him our gruel,
Yech, kraut, we said
Eat, kraut, we said
Our Russian gruel.

Too much trouble to take him
        (Seven kilometres from headquarters,
In the savage cold,
        On that shitty road)
It was a pity, of course...
But it was war, and they
Had no pity for us and burned
Our breadless cottages...
        Suddenly from behind
On the back of his head
        So we wouldn't accidentally catch
His eye before he died.

FROM

NEXT TO CHECHNYA

Рядом С Чечней

2012

The dogs of Grozny,
abandoned and evil,
Among the ruins of Grozny
with their teeth tear at the dead,
Yesterday's kings
of courtyards and discos.

· 1995 ·

Invisible spirits
Spirits of these unchristened, hostile mountains,
Descend into the valley at night,
             fall on our soldiers
And on our police

Long ago we conquered
This land of rebellion,
             but the spirits of its gorges
Have not yet forgiven us

· 2000 ·

Pkharmat Bound

A mystery play based on the Chechen myth of Prometheus.

DRAMATIS PERSONÆ:
Pkharmat, the Chechen Prometheus
Uja, the servant of the god Sela
a blacksmith
chorus of Vainakh women

The reader should imagine the highlands in the Caucasus and, chained to a rock, Pkharmat-Prometheus. The blacksmith enters. Other characters enter when joining the action.

BLACKSMITH:
By the will of almighty Sela,
father of clouds, master of the mountains
I knuckled under,
forged shackles,
unbreakable,
and chained you, great thief
To this rock of prolonged tribulation.
What could I do, Pkharmat?
I feared the immeasurable wrath
of Sela – the god of the Vainakhs
the heavenly thunderer
There was nowhere to run,
nowhere to hide
You instructed the Vainakhs
in the many manual arts, Pkharmat,
You instructed me,
and now you see here
How the fruit ripened...
My unhappy hands
have done this shameful deal
I forged a chain of torture,

not a true sword
And not a ringing shield

PKHARMAT:
Deeds of valour are the province of heroes,
and you are no hero, but a craftsman
You are guilty, of course,
but you can be forgiven, blacksmith,
For your timidity

CHORUS OF VAINAKH WOMEN:
Woe, great woe
Brought upon us by the will of Sela
you are bound to your rock, Pkharmat,
For your creative deed.
In crevices, in the caves of the earth
we lived as wild men,
Knowing nothing of fire,
We ate our meat raw, we dug the roots
of elusive plants and ate them
And wrapped ourselves in animal skins
against the long cold
It was terrible, brutish,
Drank death with our breast milk,
But you came, our saviour,
and brought the firebrand from heaven
From the hearth of the dwelling
of Sela, the god of the Vainakhs.
And suddenly our tearful life dawned
             with a new light
Glory to you, our hero.

UJA, SERVANT OF SELA:
A chorus of mourners
laments your fate

And calls you a hero, Pkharmat,
And yet you are no hero –
but a rogue, a rascal,
You lied to God, rogue,
plied him with drink and plucked a firebrand
From his hearth, you ingenious thief.
You brought down immeasurable anger,
you shifty robber, an immense wrath.
You have been punished for stealing
and your punishment is merited

PKHARMAT:
And why did the great god
Sela, the father of clouds,
So vigilantly guard
his domestic hearth
And not share his fire.
After all, the ancestors of these Vainakhs
Are the creation of his own hands
fashioned from cloudy clay
He is the father of the Vainakhs
and not just the master of their lives

UJA:
Sela, the primaeval craftsman,
Implanted a thoughtful light, an inquisitive spirit
in the primaeval skull,
The skull of the first man
This was a great gift, a gift for the ages,
that made all further gifts superfluous
For now people should
discover for themselves how to strike sparks
And how to domesticate the savage fire
Like a prisoner from Colchis to their service

PKHARMAT:
But for long and hungry ages,
hiding from the cold in caves,
The people lived seeing only occasional sparks,
Catching only lightning from heaven
thirstily with their eyes

UJA:
So the unhappy Vainakhs were proud?
Are they now happy?
Has it been so long
since glorious warriors perished in battle?
Haven't blood relatives repudiated one another
For the offences of their forefathers?

PKHARMAT:
Much grief, I know,
but when I brought the triumphing firebrand
Into an impoverished land
from the heavenly tower
The Vainakhs rejoiced

UJA:
I saw for myself how they were rejoicing,
but did their joy last long?

PKHARMAT:
Joy is fleeting.
But what of that? The cold of heaven
No longer hides in the caves of the Vainakhs
And in their homes there are hearths,
a domesticated flame, logs
From the day of creation
has there befallen a greater happiness?

UJA:
There is indeed a happier happiness:
to know, to discover, and to think for yourself
Not hoping for the help
of grasping thieves and deceivers.
This joy you deprived them of, Pkharmat.
And what's given for free
has little value

PKHARMAT:
Servant of the God Sela
why do you torment me?
Is it really too little
that every day the talons of an eagle
Tear at my body
and does he who sends that eagle
          The angry Sela
want to fill my head with doubt?

UJA:
The god does not want your torment
but only your repentance

PKHARMAT:
Repentance? For what?

UJA:
Sela is merciful:
he is ready to forgive the transgressor
If the proud thief will himself say
that what he did was not good

PKHARMAT:
I will not say so, I will not deny myself.
Thinking about battling with the heavens
Has permeated my body

and gives me the strength to bear
My daily torture.
And it is enough for me to know that the mountain villages
Honour me like a god.

UJA:
Yes, they honour, they extol you...
But are the people right to praise
a predatory deed,
valuing the craft of thievery
Over valour?
You, Pkharmat, taught them that
Among other crafts

PKHARMAT:
Vainakh women, are these words just?

CHORUS OF VAINAKH WOMEN:
An earthly audacity
became your blood and breath
You taught the Vainakhs, Pkharmat,
to be audacious and ungoverned.
Do not turn your mind
unselfish, great thief,
Pay no heed to the seductive speech of Sela's messenger
A mind free like a snow leopard in a trap
You are a hero patiently bearing your torment
and they love you as such in the mountain villages
Leader of a rebellious people, Pharmat,
do not indict yourself before Sela

PKHARMAT:
I will neither indict nor deny myself.

UJA:
Pkharmat, you were not afraid of defying

the god's prohibitions
You were not afraid of robbery,
but you are afraid to tell
the truth to these people...
Not everyone has been blinded
by the stolen firebrand...
Do not believe the chorus, listen
to what the blacksmith says

BLACKSMITH:
For me only miserable bitterness!
I am no hero, Pkharmat,
just an unhappy craftsman
I carried out the will
of the great Sela, forged chains
And for this crime they despise me in the villages
My torments
are more terrible than the eagle's talons.
My trembling hands
can no longer hold a hammer
Help me, Pkharmat,
Take the blame before Sela, Pkharmat,
And then the world will forget
My shame
          and the prideful Vainakhs in their villages
Will forgive their blacksmith

UJA:
So, Pkharmat, choose:
A considered repentance
or an endless, senseless quarrel
With the master of life

CHORUS OF VAINAKH WOMEN:
Servant of Sela the God!
A hero can not be asked to indict himself

Like a negligent slave...
A great hero should be reconciled
With the angry god as an equal

UJA:
Pkharmat is not to be equated with a god
Pkharmat is mortal, the god immortal

PKHARMAT:
I know different:
Sela himself will someday grow old
And die like us

UJA:
You lie! He is immortal
and is not to be equated with mortals
Do not be obstinate, Pkharmat,
obey his will, Pkharmat

PKHARMAT:
What's done is done.
Even if it is not right, I will not obey

UJA:
Go on, persevere, but remember:
The taloned eagle has never tired
of flying every morning

PKHARMAT:
I will remember

The End

· 2001 ·

FROM

JOB AND
THE ARAB

Иов И Араб

2013

Job and the Arab

ARAB:
Unfortunate man
now fortunate in your tent,
I have come to you, Job,
wanting to understand why
My new life, my second life,
is like a deep hole in heaven
compared with yours.
I have heard how you live at ease
with all your household
And have forgotten the Sabaeans
who slaughtered your sons,
And the shard you used to scrape your skin among the ashes,
You have long since let it go.
I, Job, I am that very Arab of the Qur'an
Who questioned God
and was punished for it and slept
Many years in the wilderness,
and then, by God's grace,
Made young again,
the pitiful bones of my donkey
Clothed again in flesh.
And I came to my own city
hoping to return to the past,
To pick up my old life,
but my wife did not recognise me
And my neighbours spurned me
saying I had been made a ghost,
A perfidious demon.
I became a beggar in the marketplace
and in this shameful guise
I have come to you, Job.

JOB:

Why do you think
me fortunate, as I was before?
God bribed me
in order to stop my cries
And forget about those slain
by bloodthirsty Sabaean swords.
But why where they afflicted?
They were not oxen and sheep
Not moving, living property...
So why did the Lord unleash a terrible power,
Reveal himself to me through death?
I do not pity myself
I do not complain that my own flesh was torn
And a multitude of sores
and boils erupted on my skin.
But my sons... Why them?
Perhaps I was guilty of something,
but what guilt was theirs?
Let someone learned and wise
explain all this to me,
If God himself chooses
to explain nothing to anyone.

ARAB:

Job, this is blasphemy...

JOB:

No, I want justice.
I want truth, without that,
Wine is not wine to me,
bread is not bread,
life is not life. But tell
Why you have come to my tent
to reprove me.

ARAB:
What else can a beggar do?
His only pleasure
Is to reprove the prosperous.

JOB:
Yes, I am indeed prosperous...
Yet a slow and ancient venom
Nourishes my brain ever since
I sat among the ashes.
I take no delight in showy peacocks
And strutting ostriches...
Nor do I want to return
To my former, thoughtless life...
A poisoned wisdom
Has replaced all pleasure.

ARAB:
And yet I still believe
God is sure to restore
My former happiness.

JOB:
He gave you back your youth
and nothing more.
Do not wish for any going back.
Try to live a new life.
And I will help you.

ARAB:
Very well. I will try.

FROM

ON THE MUDDY RIVER

На Реку Непрозрачной

2005

On the muddy river
       some kind of cruddy boat
Stains of some kind of slime,
       condoms floating
Under the bridges to the bay
       past warehouses, hospitals, garages
And the half-rotted head
       of an Orpheus-busker
Who sang off-key in the metro

· 2003 ·

Philemon and Baucis
  in their own creaking hovel,
On their own burnt-over patch of land
  across from the new mcmansion,
Wait to be swept away by a storm –
  a private liquidation,
To clear the countryside.

· 2003 ·

Robert Oppenheimer at the First Test of the Atom Bomb

This poem is an imagined conversation of Robert Oppenheimer with General Groves on 16 July 1945, at the first test in history of the atom bomb at Alamagordo, New Mexico. It is well known that at the moment of the explosion Oppenheimer recalled verses from the Bhagavad-Gita: the appearance of the God Krishna to the warrior Arjuna in his own true appearance.

At Alamagordo, on the field of dharma
Night is black in the hour before the dawn

'What's that awful music! Cut it out!
Some kind of dancing tra-la-la-la...
     it's vile... trash... stop it'

'Shut it down, Johnny' – 'Yes, sir' – Quiet.
Night is black in the hour before the dawn
at Alamagordo, on the field of dharma

Where does this weakness in you come from,
Arjuna, at this time of crisis?
It is not fitting in a nobleman. It does not gain you heaven.
It does not bring you any honour.

'In Göttingen, I recall a puny little student
In Aryan studies,
     with a hellish madness in his eyes...
There were just those kinds
     of people in power in Berlin not so long ago'

'Sir, it's morning... Time to begin. We're ready.'

'He was a splendid scholar, but he was, I think,
Fully capable of making a bomb for Hitler.

Not for nothing he respectfully
Talked about it with Niels.'

'Sir, we're ready...'
Arjuna spoke:
Krishna, if you think that insight
Is more powerful than action,
Then why do you urge me
To engage in such a terrible action as this?

'Sir, we're starting...'

If the light of a thousand suns
Were to suddenly arise in heaven –
As at the dawn of a new age –
That would be like the radiance of this great soul!

'Groves, this is terrible!' 'This means victory, professor.'

I see your body as it touches the clouds, shining a rainbow of colours,
Your large gaping mouth, your wide flaming eyes.
My inmost self trembles.
I cannot find my resolve, Vishnu. I cannot find peace.

I see your mouths and your wide gaping tusks
That look to me like the fires at the end of time.
I am disoriented now and can find no shelter.
Krishna, lord of the gods and the world's repose, have mercy!

'Sir, I shake your hand. We have won today.
Fear will bring the enemy to reason,
        Terror will save the warring world.
Thousands of our boys,
        having escaped slaughter, will soon

Return to their families...
        We have saved them today,
Having awakened the power of the atom'

I am become death, Arjuna

O the holocaust in Oświęcim
The accusation of a documentary film
　　　　　　is interrupted by an advertisement
For the very latest cosmetics
　　　　　　from the collection of a screen diva
A fashionable caprice
　　　　　　shoves its way into the death zone

What's in the collection?
　　　　　　Eau de cologne for behind the ears
henna for the hair of the Lorelei
　　　　　　powder for the cheek of Marguerite

Little bottles of nail polish,
　　　　　　and compacts with the cremated ashes
Ashes of the bones of the Shulamite

What's with Russia? A turn to the West?
Will the smell of the back stairway
Finally dissipate,

The smell of the psychiatric ward,
        the depression of those faces
That wasting gloom
        finally disappear?

· 2003 ·

Russophobia

The Russian Russophobe rushes to the river – to drown
('Fed up with living in this eternal vile squalor!')
But reconsiders: there is a choice – to emigrate,
Or (variation on a theme): to express in hellishly
Contemptuous verse his heartfelt, furious heat...

Which published, brings him a substantial fee

· 2003 ·

The Italian Rooms at the Hermitage

Umbrian dreams are a Russian ark,
  windows opening on azure hills,
But in the windows across the way:
  a Nevsky gloom, Stygian ice,
murky snow
  and on the far shore, behind the blizzard,
The prison of all Russia. The hard mouth
Of cold cells.

· 2003 ·

The 'Trinity' of Rublev

Those three came to Abram
      Three holy ones of few words,
Wandering and tired...
      Staffs in their slender hands,
Heads slightly bent, a chiming
      Of bells in the field, in the rye...

· 1998 ·

After an Exhibition of Filonov

Such strength in an iconoclast?
In the trapezoidal goblets,
     in the squareblack bread?
In the rustyiron fish
     on the gimcrack table?
What kind of dark strength
     in the distorted faces of the diners
at the mystic meal?

· 1993 ·

FROM

REVIVAL OF
A TAMBOURINE

Оживление Бубна

2009

The Mountain Sary-Tau

a narrative drawn from one of the subjects of the Tatar epic Idegäy

We stood together on the steppe at midnight,
My friend, not to return, not to look back.

— Blok, 'On the field of Kulikovo'

1

'Great Khan, Seyid Ahmad has returned from Ukek and wants to see you.'

Khan Toktamysh had only just risen from his prayer rug and, hearing these words from the doorkeeper, hurried toward the entrance of the Golden Yurt. According to custom, the Khan himself had to go to meet Seyid, a man learned in the laws and will of Allah. In the courtyard of the Altyn-Tash – the Golden Courtyard – which spread out behind the Golden Yurt, Toktamysh saw two *kibitkas* – tented wagons: one rich, belonging to Seyid, and another, much more modest. Seyid's tent was white felt embroidered with green crescent moons fringed with pearls. The *arbakesh* who was sitting on the goats was wearing a green satin coat, very dusty after a long journey. The second *kibitka* was grey, and its arbakesh also wore something grey and nondescript. Toktamysh approached the white *kibitka*, threw back the curtains, and helped Seyid Ahmad climb down. Then, following custom, he kissed his hand.

'I am not alone today, great Khan,' said Seyid Ahmat. 'With me is Bey Durmen from Ukek. He has business to take up with you.'

'I know Bey Durmen. He is a courageous warrior and an honest man. What is his business?'

'His son Urman has been executed. He has arrested the executioner and brought him to you for judgement, Great Khan.'

'Bring him before me.'

In the grey *kibitka* there was movement, and from it emerged Bey Durmen, a man of a venerable age; and after him a boy of thirteen or fourteen, with his hands bound. The frightened teenager stared at Toktamysh.

'Is this the one?' Toktamysh wondered aloud.

'The very one, Great Khan,' Bey Durmen confirmed. 'He cut off the head of my son Urman.'

'Bring him before me. We will pass judgement right now.'

Toktamysh returned with the Seyid to the *kibitka*, and Bey Durmen took the boy by the collar and dragged him to the threshold. There he unbuckled his own sword and laid it to the left of the entrance.

'Untie the boy, Bey,' said the doorkeeper.

'No,' said Durmen. 'He is the murderer of my son and not worthy of pity.'

The doorkeeper drew back the curtain and both Durmen and his prisoner went in to the Khan. The Khan's yurt was made of white felt and called Golden because it rested on golden pillars and was ornamented with a great number of golden plaques. In the yurt there was a wooden throne ornamented in silver – the Khan took it with him into battle, while his main throne ornamented in gold stayed in the palace where Toktamysh received foreign ambassadors. When Durmen and the boy walked in, Toktamysh was already installed on the throne. To his right on a long bench sat Seyid Ahmad and the *karachi* – men of noble birth with whom the Khan took counsel and regulated the court.

'Untie the boy, Bey,' Toktamysh commanded. Durmen obeyed.

'What is your name, boy?'

'Beket.'

'Beket, why did you kill Durmen's son?'

'The guilt is not mine, great Khan. It was Kubugyl who ordered me to execute Urman.'

'Kugubyl? The son of Jantimir?'

'Yes, Great Khan.'

'This Kubugyl was disrespectful to me when I crossed the lands of the Manghuds. He is an impudent and wilful youth. But of what was Urman guilty?'

'He stole wooden horses from the children of nobles. They

were brought to us by Russian merchants, and many important people bought them for their children. But Urman wanted to have the whole herd at home for himself, and he began stealing them. Three times he succeeded, but he was caught the fourth time, and then Kubugyl called us together...'

'Who is this *us*?'

'The children of the nobles, Great Khan. Kubugyl had mustered the sons of these families and become our ataman. Then he asked Bey Burluk to teach us archery and the use of the sword.

'Are you listening, Seyid?' Toktamysh turned to Seyid Ahmad.

'He is a dangerous one, this Kubugyl,' answered Ahmad.

'Go on with your story, Beket.'

'Kubugyl called us together and said that Urman had to be executed, because that was the custom of our ancestors. Then he took me aside and said, "Beket, you have a steady hand. You handle a sword better than all the others. I instruct you to do so."'

Toktamysh thought about this. He understood that the boy was only carrying out the orders of Kubugyl and should not be executed. But the self-willed son of Jantimir must also not be left without attention.

'What do you say about this, Bey Kutuz?' He turned to one of the *karachi*, a renowned warrior no longer young.

'I say that Kubugyl was right. He acted in accordance with the custom and the law of your realm, Great Khan. A horse thief has to be executed.'

'But these were not real horses,' countered Toktamysh.

'Evil should be rooted out when it is still a young shoot. If you let it grow strong, it will bring down your dominion, Khan.'

'Great Khan,' Bey Durmen interrupted. 'I have always been your faithful servant. I lost my only son. Let this boy pay with his head for the head of Urman.'

'Bey Durmen,' Toktamysh said. 'You have always served me faithfully and I realise how great is your grief. But the punishment should not be as evil as the crime, otherwise there will be no justice in my realm. Let Seyid Ahmad say how the boy should be punished.'

'Fifty lashes of the knout, Great Khan.'

'Let it be so,' Toktamysh said. 'If he survives fifty blows and remains alive, it is the will of Allah.'

Durmen was clearly unhappy with this turn of events, but did not dare to contradict the Khan and only asked permission to be present at the punishment.

'No,' said Toktamysh. 'Bey, you should rest after your journey. My servant will bring you to the palace. Dwell with me for a few days, it is long since I have seen you.'

Durmen bowed and, accompanied by servants of the Khan, went out of the yurt.

'Seyid Ahmad,' Toktamysh said immediately after his departure, 'this boy will not survive fifty lashes. If he dies, the Manghuds will hold it against us.'

'We have to punish him, Great Khan. Otherwise Kubugyl will think that we endorse his execution of Urman.'

'You are right, Seyid. I suggest ten lashes and then we send him home.'

'But what will we say to Durmen?'

'We will tell Durmen that Beket survived the fifty lashes and, by the will of Allah, is still alive.'

Seyid Ahmad agreed. A servant led Beket beside the Golden Yurt to punish him. The Khan Toktamysh occupied himself with Seyid and the *karachi* in the affairs of the realm; and, when the servant came back, he asked:

'Did he cry out?'

'No, Great Khan. Not a single sound.'

'So, when he becomes an *azamat* he will make a good warrior. Now, tell me, is there a caravan leaving for Ukek tomorrow?'

'Yes, Great Khan. The caravan of Bukhara leaves your capital tomorrow morning.'

'Good. Take the boy to them and have them take him home. We will tell Bey Durmen that he ran away.'

The next morning Beket left Sarai Berke with the Bukhara caravan.

2

The place of execution was beyond the town on the banks of the Idil near the mountain Sary-Tau. In that place used to stand, according to the stories of the elders, a *tiyak* – a sacrificial stone on which they sacrificed the firstborn of the herds. That was in the old days, when the Manghuds worshiped their own dark gods, before they adopted the true faith of the Prophet Muhammad. Now there was a scaffold on the spot, where they beheaded those who violated the law and customs of their ancestors. It was early morning, the sun had just risen above the Idil and was lighting up the mountainside. His hands bound, Urman kneeled in front of the block, his doomed face turned down to it. Standing apart in expectation were the children of noble families, and before them, inflexible and imperious, with an axe on his shoulder – Kubugyl.

'Beket, come here,' he commanded.

The boy approached the ataman, who handed him the axe.

'You have a steady hand, Beket,' he said. 'You must be the one to do it.'

Beket felt his arms and legs go numb, but he ordered himself to be a man, approached Urman and slowly began to raise the axe. At this very moment as if a bolt of lightning had passed through his body, he cried out loudly... and woke up.

He woke up in his parents' home, in a large upper room, on a sleeping-couch, framed by three walls. Awakened by his screaming, his entire family crowded in: parents, brothers, sisters, and other relatives.

'Are you drunk, from the *tarasun* you drank?' his father asked.

They were all hung over from the fermented milk they had imbibed the day before in celebration of the safe return of Beket from Sarai Berke, and in praise of the Khan Toktamysh for a fair trial. Leaning over him especially was the visiting Bey Burluk: the boy was his favourite student.

'I had a bad dream,' Beket said. 'Nothing to do with the *tarasun*.'

'Did you dream they executed you?'

'Not me. Urman.'

'Urman deserved his death. You have nothing to regret.'

The following night, the same thing happened. Beket again screamed and struggled in his bed on the sleeping-couch. In the morning, his father went for advice to the mullah.

'An evil spirit has possessed him,' the mullah said. 'You will have to exorcise the evil spirit, Bey. Take *bayalych* and fumigate the sleeping chamber at sunset. And here are scarves for you, cover Beket with them before he goes to sleep.

He showed the scarves embroidered with Arabic writing.

'What is embroidered here?' asked the father.

'The one hundred thirteen suwar of the Qur'an. They will chase away impure spirits.'

However, no herbs for fumigation nor embroidered scarves helped. The fit was even stronger than before. In the morning, when the men drank their *koumiss* in a yurt standing in the courtyard, one of Beket's brothers offered to send him to the north, to Atryach, to the famous *kama* Bayan, whose fame as a healer was spoken of all through the Horde.

'The mullah will be displeased,' the father said. But all the same his sons persuaded him, and it was decided to send Beket to Atryach with the next caravan. When they rose up from the carpet and began to go out of the tent, Ilya, a Russian slave assigned to serve at meals, plucked at Beket's sleeve. He had the build and bearing of a noble warrior, and usually said little.

'Stay, Beket. I have something to tell you.'

Beket remained. Ilya first drank off the left-over *koumiss* in the wooden bowls (left there for the servant) and then said:

'I know why you scream at night. You dream about how you cut off Urman's head.'

'Yes,' confirmed Beket.

'The sin is on you. And the *kama* Bayan will not help you.' (The word *sin* Ilya said in Russian.)

'What does it mean, *sin?*'

'The sin is the blood of Urman that you shed. This blood has not disappeared. It torments you, and will continue to torment you.'

'What can I do, Ilya?'

'Expiate the sin in prayer. But this can be done only among us in Russia, in a monastery.'

'And what is a monastery?'

'A monastery is a place where people live who have dedicated themselves to God. They pray for us, for our salvation. I used to live in a village near a monastery like this. The abbot, Father Joseph, will take you in if you turn to him.'

'But how do I get there?'

'That's not so hard. Right now, Russian merchants have come to Ukek with their trade goods. They are from just this very place. I have come to an agreement with them, and they will take you and me back. But you will tell your family that they are taking you to Atryach.'

'But how will I explain what I need? I speak no Russian.'

'Father Joseph speaks Tatar. It is said that, before he became an abbot, he lived in Sarai Berke with a young prince of the Khan's court.

Beket thought hard, excited by the proposal of the Russian slave. And then suddenly, unexpectedly even for himself, he said,

'Listen, Ilya. You're a strong fellow, a real *bogatyr*. You remember, Bey Burluk proposed to buy you from my father, because he wanted you as a fighter in the Khan's army. But you refused then. Why? Weren't you attracted by a life of freedom?'

'Of course I was tempted. But I heard here in Ukek what it would be like. This was a long time ago, in the days when the Khan Tokta made war against the Khan Nogai. They were fighting to see who would rule the Golden Horde. Tokta defeated the army of Nogai and scattered it. Nogai escaped and a Russian fighter went after him. Nogai was already old and felt his strength leaving him, and he turned to the fighter.

'"Don't kill me," he said. "I am powerless and I can not fight with you as an equal. Do not kill me, take me to Tokta."

'But the fighter killed him and cut off his head. He sent the head to Tokta, hoping for praise and reward.

'"How did you kill Nogai?" asked Tokta.

'The fighter told him.

'"You wretch," cried Tokta bitterly. "You dared to kill an old man begging you for mercy. You have earned no reward but death."

'And they executed the fighter.'

'You're afraid the same thing can happen to you?' asked Beket, but Ilya said nothing. He kept his promise and agreed with the Russian merchants that the boy would be taken to Russia. After a few days, on an anxious morning, Beket said goodbye to his family and to Bey Burluk on the riverbank, by the merchants' fleet. A cold wind blew and an oppressive black storm cloud hung over the Idil. They wished him a good recovery, asked him to come home soon, and it was unbearably hard for Beket to lie that he would soon return, freed by *kama* Bayan from the torment of the evil spirit. And only when the fleet had already sailed far away, and the mountain of Sary-Tau was barely visible, did Beket finally realise that he would never return to Ukek. He understood and wept like a little boy. After just two weeks the fleet crossed the western border of the Golden Horde.

'And here is Russia,' said one of the oarsmen.

3

The Russian city where the merchants brought Beket was situated on the shore of the Idil where it was not so wide as in his homeland. On a hill towered a white stone fortress, where, as they told Beket, a prince lived, and the city itself was all wood, unlike the stone and adobe Ukek. It was larger than Ukek, but certainly smaller than Sarai Berke with its more than eighty streets and gardens. The merchants sailed to the Grand Bazaar on the river bank and began to unload their goods. Becket said goodbye to each of his companions, and a young merchant whom he had befriended during the voyage undertook to show him the monastery. It was hot and Beket wanted a drink, but to his surprise the bazaar did not have a single fountain. When he learned what Beket wanted, the young merchant led him to a man who was selling something to drink. The drink proved refreshing and slightly sour. Beket learned later that it was kvass.

They quickly found a shop where an old but lively monk sold

bast shoes embroidered by the monks. Beket's travelling companion began to explain something to the monk, and although, after a fortnight of sailing the boy had begun to understand the Russian language and even speak in Russian, many of the words in their conversation were incomprehensible to him. During their conversation the old man looked with curiosity at the *ordynchik* (as they called him) and then, collecting his unsold sandals and locking up his shop, told Beket that he would take him into the monastery. Beket embraced his friend when they parted, expressing the hope that they would meet again, and followed the monk. It had rained not long before, and in the city streets were wide sunny puddles of drying mud, in which chickens swarmed. Here and there, elderberries winked from behind fences.

The old man, who was walking in front, cleverly picked out the drier spots and deftly jumped over the puddles. However, he kept muttering, either praying or just talking to himself. Suddenly the city ended, broad meadows began and, beyond the meadows hills were visible covered with forests.

'*Black spruce*,' the monk said, pointing to the forest. 'And the monastery is not far beyond.'

When they came to the forest, the road began to rise into the hills.

'Close now. There's Saint Paraskeva, right at the bend, and past the bend, a stone's throw. We'll take a rest at Paraskeva,' the old man continued.

Up ahead, where the road bent to the left, stood a post with an icon under a cover. Suddenly, two monks came out of the woods up to the post with bundles of wood, and, dropped these to the ground, and sat down on a log beside the post.

'Here is our abbot, and with him the father-cellarer.'

When they caught up, the old man came for a blessing to the tall monk with a hard and imperious face, his whole appearance more like a warrior than a man of prayer. Beket immediately guessed that this was Father Joseph, about whom Ilya had told him. After the blessing, Beket's companion pointed to him:

'Here is the *mussulman lad*, the one who wants to taste our honey.'

The abbot looked searchingly at the boy.

'Where are you from?' he asked in the Tatar language.

'From Ukek.'

'Manghud?'

'Yes.'

'What decided you to come to us?'

'Sin,' answered Beket, using the Russian word he had learned from Ilya. 'I was an executioner,' he clarified.

Father Joseph was not surprised.

'You have done right, coming to us. We are the only ones who can help you. Let's go, you will live with us.'

The abbot and the father-cellarer stood up from the log, crossed themselves in devotion to the image of Saint Paraskeva and shouldered once again their bundles of firewood.

'Let me carry your wood, *ata*,' suggested Beket.

'No,' Father Joseph cut him off sharply. 'This is obedience,' he added in Russian.

'Did someone command you to this, *ata*?'

'God so commanded.'

After Paraskeva the road turned to the left and steeply downward. Soon, on the right, beyond a green web of birches, a lake glittered in the gaps between their trunks, and on the shore the monastery was visible, fabulously beautiful, domes bathed in the light of a blissful heaven. A feeling of approaching holiday and at the same time an inexplicable anxiety swept over Beket. He sensed the beginning of a new life for him, quite unlike his old one. The road down to the shore of lake, smelling of muck. Right by the water stood a black log hut with a single little window. The old monk held Beket by his sleeve:

'There is the devil's wash-house. A demon lives there.'

The abbot and the cellarer, walking ahead of them, turned sharply:

'Have you seen it?' Father Joseph asked.

'Not I. Others have seen it.'

'Then do not say that it's a demon...'

The road began to wind among the thick grass, nearer the monastery, and finally, the travellers entered through a large wooden gate and were on the square in front of the church. A crowd was gathered at the church: monks, pilgrims, peasants from surrounding villages. Beket immediately noticed boys in the crowd: one his age and others even younger: these were the *golyshny* – orphans living at the monastery. Father Joseph and the cellarer dropped their firewood, and went up to the water barrel. Beside the barrel a novice stood with a bucket and a towel. After a blessing the novice washed the hands of the abbot, the cellarer, and then the old monk.

Beckett approached and saw that the waterer gave him a hateful look. He stretched out his hands, but the novice casually splashed the water on his feet. Father Joseph frowned.

'Pour again,' he said, and, when the novice poured the water properly, he added, 'You will be punished.'

They all went into the church, and the service began. Beket was stunned. The church with its multitude of candle lights and incomprehensible images on the walls and the icon-screens seemed to him the magic cave of a fairy tale. The singing made a strong impression on him, although they sang in liturgical language, and almost all the words were incomprehensible. After the service, everyone who lived in the monastery walked, singing 'Praise the Lord, my soul,' into a long wooden building, the refectory. There three tables were speedily set, one for brethren and novices, another for the employees and pilgrims, and a third small one where they placed Beket – for the *golyshny*. They lit the lamp in the corner before the Virgin Mary and a young monk, standing beside it, began to read something from a book in the same incomprehensible language. Beket learned later that it was the life of the saint honoured on this day. The meal itself was meagre: pea soup with diced bread and a mug of the kvass he was already familiar with. Later, it's true, they provided more and milk porridge for two of the three tables – but not for the monks. It was forbidden to talk while eating, which clearly annoyed the *golyshny*. But they had devised a game, which they probably repeated every day: as soon as the monk in charge of the *golyshny* closed his eyes (nodding off to sleep) a salvo of bread balls were shot up to the ceiling, and each *golyshnya* watched to see whose ball stuck to the ceiling.

After the meal, singing 'How amiable are thy tabernacles, O Lord of hosts!' everyone went out into the courtyard. Father Joseph approached Beket and said he should come with him to his cell.

The cells in the monastery were ugly little log houses with one little window, only the father abbot's cell had two windows. In a large stove birch firewood burned with a fresh smell. A lamp burned in front of the image of Our Lady of the Way.

'Sit down, tell me your story,' said Father Joseph.

Beket sat on a bench and began his story. When he had finished, the abbot stayed silent for a little, then spoke this time in Russian:

'Your Kubugyl is a like an animal, a child of Hagar, thick-headed. But his time will come – he will be melted in the fiery womb. And you, young man, God took note of you. Live with us and wait for the sign that our Lord has forgiven you. And the sign will be when you accept holy baptism.'

'What does baptism mean, *ata*?'

'How can I explain it to you... Today you saw the bathing place at the lake. That is where our monks wash. True, we have some who do not wash, they say that washing indulges the devil... Such thinking is wrong, because the body, like the soul, is from God. So there is one bath for the external body, and there is another bath for the soul. That one is called baptism. It washes away all sin. As King David sang of the Lord: "I shall be washed whiter than snow."'

'Tell me, *ata*, after I am baptised, may I go back to Ukek?'

'No, never. From today there is no way back. You will accept the light into your heart, but your home will remain in darkness.'

'But don't they also believe in God?'

'You can believe in different ways.. They believe in God with the heart, that's what an animal does. Yet the Lord does not want faith alone, but also love, and hope.'

'If the Russian faith is best,' Beket was not convinced, 'why do you pay tribute to our Khan?'

Father Joseph thought about that.

'You are not the first to ask this question,' he said. 'I asked about this, and Seyid Ahmad and the Khan himself asked me about this when I was a young prince in your capital, New Sarai. I did not know what to say then, but now I do. We Russians are workers of the eleventh hour and called by the Lord in the end of times. The Mordovians, the Komi, the people of Perm, have a forest-heart. You Tatars have a steppe-heart, and our heart is in the Lord's own hands. And thus our work is to bring light into the darkness of the forest and the darkness of the steppe. To us, Russians, this light has been given freely, by the great mercy of God. But the Lord saith, "Work, earn it." And he gives our people a test, and watches: Will we pass it or not. And this is our test, being subject to the Horde. Yes, we are humbled , but in our humility our spirit grows. The time will come, and it is already near, when our princes will unite and refuse to pay tribute to the ruler of the Horde. It will be a great battle, but our side will prevail, and the Khan will then take our faith. And after him his people will take it. Do you understand everything I'm saying?'

'Not everything, *ata*,' confessed Beket. Many of your words are incomprehensible to me.'

'Well, it doesn't matter. Eventually you will understand what's important: you are on the first step of the *Ladder of Divine Ascent...*'

'What is this *Ladder, ata*?'

'The *Ladder of Divine Ascent* is an invisible ladder, a stairway toward God. You have acknowledged your sin, which means you have taken the first step. There will be a second. And in order to help you climb it, I will give you a first prayer. It is very simple: "Lord Jesus Christ, son of God, have mercy on me." Repeat it seven times.'

Beket repeated it.

'That's how you will pray. Pray out loud, so that the devils can hear it and tremble. But this not everything. Do not hold a grudge against Andrey...'

'Who is Andrey?'

'The one who splashed water on your feet. His father was a captive of the Tatars, and they did violence to his mother. So he hates all of you. But you, you will ask God to soften his heart. This is hard, I know, but without forgiveness there is no true faith. And now, go, child. You will live in the dormitory of the *golyshni*, right next to the refectory. You will work with us, and, when God gives the sign, you will be baptised. The abbot blessed the boy and Beket went off to the dormitory where the orphans lived. Near the church he met Andrey who, seeing him, spat and said something nasty.

'Could he be Ilya's son?' thought Beket.

4

A morning, chilly sun had risen over the river Idil and lit the cliffs of the mountain Sary-Tau, the monotonous coastal grass and a wooden chopping block on the shore. In that place used to stand, according to the stories of the elders, a *tiyak* – a sacrificial stone on which they sacrificed the firstborn of the herds. Urman, with his hands bound, dropped to his knees and turned his face to the sacrificial wooden block. The noble boys stood aloof and silent. Beket approached Urman and raised the axe he was holding, but at that moment someone's invisible hand stopped his own hand. Beket turned and saw behind him an unknown boy. He was dressed in white felt and had an extraordinarily beautiful face without Manghud features. An angel, Beket guessed, and he turned to look at Kubugyl. Kubugyl, who had just looked so moody and important, suddenly beamed.

'The execution is cancelled. God has pardoned Urman,' he said. And here Beket woke up.

The damp autumn dawn barely penetrated the bull bladders on the windows. Not yet called to morning prayer, the *golyshny* and their chaperone slept blissfully. Beket would have liked to wake them up and tell them about his dream. He had already lived a month in the monastery, and, during that time, he had not dreamed once of Urman's execution. He had quickly established good relations with the *golyshny*; they were almost all younger and weaker than he. His only age-mate, the chosen ringleader, had tried bullying him but was beaten in the very first fight. The orphans recognised the primacy of the *ordynchik* and respected him immensely because he knew how to ride a horse and how to handle a sword and a bow. The monks and novices, except for Andrey who continued to watch him like a wolf, also took to Beket sympathetically; besides, everyone knew that the abbot was his patron, and that the abbot himself would be the one to baptise him.

They were called to morning prayers. The orphans and their chaperone woke up. After a short prayer they all washed up at the water barrel, standing by the door in the courtyard. There was no time to hear about the dream, they rushed into the church. After morning prayers, Beket went to Father Joseph and told him his dream.

'You see, God has given you a sign,' said the abbot. 'you are already on the second step of the *Ladder*, it will be easier to go further. Today I will baptise you. Your name will no longer be Beket, you will be the novice Joasaph.'

'Why will I be Joasaph?'

'There was a prince in the land of India. He was brought up as a heathen, he knew nothing about the Lord. But the Lord sent him the elder Barlaam and this holy man instructed him in our faith.'

'Tell me, *ata*, can my parents and my brothers be saved?'

'If you will pray for them, the Lord will have mercy.'

'And can I pray for the Bey Burluk?'

'Yes, but the prayers of another do not save a man, only his own prayers can do that. I do not know God's plan for the Muslims. Perhaps their children or grandchildren will be saved, if they take our faith.'

'And if they do not?'

'The word of God is stronger than the sword. The khan permits the building of a monastery in his dominion, thousands are converted. Those who aren't converted are a dry branch, for the burning.'

On that same day, Father Joseph baptised Beket, and from then on he became the novice Joasaph, but, as it was difficult for many to pronounce this name, they came to call him Asaph. The abbot declared that he would be his confessor. He undertook to teach him Slavonic, and Beket-Joasaph soon began to read ecclesiastical books and to appreciate the craft of the scribe. This also gave him a special position in the monastery; the novices were all illiterate and only a few of the monks could read and write. About a future of his becoming a tonsured monk Father Joseph said nothing, and when the new novice asked him about it, replied:

'Decide for yourself. It is possible to serve God in the world, although, in my opinion, there is no better way than the monastic one.'

The more Joasaph learned about his spiritual father, the more he admired him. There had been no one like him in the Horde. According to father Joseph, monastic life was supposed to be a continuous ascent to God; but the monk, he also believed, should not be too distant from the world. 'The gateway to the world,' he said, 'must be held open. A people who look at the monastic model will themselves grow better.' The abbot counted prayer and labour as the principal elements of monastic life. 'Work in hand, prayer in mouth,' was one of his favourite sayings.

Under him, the monastery operated as a self-sufficient manor; it contained a carpentry shop, a cooperage, a workshop for weaving bast, an apple orchard (which the monks called 'Paradise') an apiary, and – outside the walls, fields. Everything that was manufactured, cultivated, and harvested was either sold at a profit or stored for a 'rainy day.' Father Joseph personally managed all the economic affairs, and the monastery prospered under him. When he was accused of money-grubbing, he usually answered, 'I acquire in order to distribute, but the person who has nothing can distribute nothing.'

And, indeed, during years of famine the monastery opened its storehouses and fed half the principality. Money also did not lie dead in his treasury: Father Joseph used it to redeem many people from their captivity in the Horde. He regarded desert-dwelling hermit monks with some suspicion, and, although he did not reject them, he said this:

'They go into the desert to hear what God has to say. But, once you've heard, don't keep the secret: go to the people and tell them what you've heard.'

From strangers who had lived a long time in the community,

Joasaph learned that other monasteries live and pray differently. He was especially disturbed in his conversation with one pilgrim, about whom it was said that he had visited the holy Mount Athos. In the monastery they nicknamed this pilgrim a *drydrunk* because of the strangeness of his speech and his piercing, testing way of looking at a person. Once Beket was sawing firewood with the *drydrunk*, and, when he read a prayer out loud during a break, the stranger said to him,

'You are pray wrong.'

'Why wrong?'

'There is another kind of prayer, internal. That's how the monks at Athos pray. An external prayer is like a leaf – in the autumn it shrivels and falls. But internal prayer is fruit.'

'And how do I create such a prayer?'

'In the morning when you rise, sit on a bench and empty your entire mind from your head into your heart. Keep it in your heart, bowing and repeating mentally, 'Lord Jesus Christ, Son of God, have mercy on me.' And keep on repeating until you feel a pain in your chest. Do not fear the pain. Light comes through it, and that light comes from God. Do you understand?'

'No, I do not understand. What does it mean to empty your mind from your head into your heart? Isn't your mind always in your head?'

'I feel it, but I can not explain it. But I can say it a different way: when our Lord Jesus Christ was on Mount Tabor, everything was shining with a miraculous light. And we should multiply our treasure, and embrace that light.'

Later, Joasaph repeated this conversation to the abbot, and asked him if he knew about internal prayer.

'I know,' answered Father Joseph. 'They pray one way, we pray another. The important thing is to pray. It's just that we do not ask God's mercy for ourselves alone, but for all the land that God delivered for us from the rule of the children of Hagar. And our labour is also for it, for the earth. Building a church, planting a garden, feeding the hungry – all these are pleasing to the Lord. And which praying is better is not for us to judge.'

The abbot fell silent, and then asked:

'Tell me, Asaph, Andrey still bears you ill will, as before.'

'Yes, *ata*. Every day I pray for the softening of his heart, but he hates me just as much.'

'It is hard for him, Asaph. He can not forgive those... And for him, you are one of them.'

'What can I do, *ata*?'

'Nothing. God has ravelled this. God will unravel it.'

And indeed, soon enough it was unravelled.

5

Several years passed. Joasaph took the tonsure and became a *conventual* – as they were called in the monastery. As before, his chief labour was copying books. He no longer thought of his life outside the walls of the monastery, but this ended as abruptly as it had begun. Suddenly, without any advance notice, the prince paid a visit to the monastery. Indeed, he often visited the monastery, but this was usually known in advance and, if the day was not a fast-day, they baked pies with fish and mushrooms for his arrival, and therefore the brothers loved these visits. But this time, the prince came at the very end of the meal and was obviously concerned about something. He shut himself up with the abbot in his cell and they talked a long time together, then he mounted his horse and galloped away with his servants, without even having glanced into the church. Joasaph, who had returned after the meal to his own cell, took up his usual book-work: with a thin brush he began to draw a heavenly branch to illuminate the initial at the beginning of the first line of the Gospel of John. And then Andrey appeared at his door:

'The abbot is asking for you, Asaph.'

Before this, Andrey had never come to him and in general avoided any communication. But for the first time his look and his voice were not hostile. 'Something has happened,' thought Joasaph and hurried to father Joseph. After a blessing, the abbot immediately took up the matter at hand.

'A momentous affair,' he said. 'The Moscow Grand Prince has refused to pay tribute to the Horde, and now the ruler Yedigei is preparing war against us.'

'Yedigei,' exclaimed Joasaph. 'I have heard about him. This is Kubugyl, he used to go by the name Kubugyl. He has overthrown the Khan Toktamysh.'

'Yes, it is he, but that's not what I'm talking about. Our *otchich*, our overlord, is an ally of the Moscow Prince and is gathering an army to meet Yedigey's. He needs *cowled* warriors, warrior-monks, who can inspire the rest of the army. At first I sent for Andrey, but the prince, knowing that Andrey had never held a sword in his hand, turned him away. And then I thought of you...'

'Me!'

'Yes, you. You yourself have told me that you handled a sword better than all the youth in Ukek.'

'But that was in another life, *ata*. I am a monk, and the business of a monk is to pray, not to fight.'

'A monk is permitted to fight. Saint Sergey sent two from his own community into battle against Mamai. Because the battle was for the faith and for our land. And our land is sacred.'

'But Yedigey is a Manghud, *ata*. In his army there will be my brothers, even Bey Burluk... I can not make war against them, *ata*.'

'It is not necessary for you to hate them. It has been a long time since they were kin to you. When you were baptised, you became ours. Empty out your heart, free yourself from an attachment to your old home. And then the spirit of Christ will enter into you.'

'I can not do that, *ata*,' Joasaph answered quietly.

'You can!' Father Joseph was practically shouting, and his face turned cruel and angry. Joasaph had never seen him like this. 'You can! I am your spiritual father and you must submit yourself to me. Tomorrow morning you will go into the city. There, in the fortress, the army is gathering. The prince is expecting you.'

Then followed a heavy, tortured silence for both of them. The abbot broke it first. He took down from the wall the image of Our Lady of the Way.

'Here is my blessing, Asaph. I will pray for you.'

'I will be killed, *ata*.'

'You may be killed, if that is the will of God. If you are killed, you will enter Paradise.'

'I already live in Paradise, *ata*. This cloister has been a Paradise for me.'

Joasaph received the blessing, said farewell, and left. He returned to his cell, and tried to continue his work on the illumination, but could not. Darkness fell, he lay down to sleep. On this night he dreamed again about the mountain Sary-Tau and the shore of the Idil. Urman was kneeling, with his bound hands and his face turned down onto the block. He, Beket, took the axe in his hand and approached Urman. Before he lifted the axe, he turned. There was no angel at his shoulder. The noble boys stood in silence and the narrow, evil eyes of Kubugyl looked at him.

'Now, yes, you,' Kubugyl said.

FROM

GRAFFITI

Граффити

2011

This really occurred: playing at revolution
   in an undernourished kindergarten:
A holocaust of toys
   and then, storming the Winter Palace
in the neighbouring garden...
A lather of passion, a snowball fight
   and hanging the traitor Venka
Right there – on a branch.

Graffiti on Victory Square

Russia saved the Georgians
        from warmongers
Saved them from catastrophe
        probably, assuredly...
That's how it happened,
        although in Russian villages
They had no idea
        and didn't think to think about it.

Russia saved the Armenians
        from Ottoman violence
Saved them from catastrophe
        probably, assuredly...
That's how it happened,
        even though recruits from the countryside
knew nothing about it,
        they still fought bravely
Beyond the Caucasus Mountains.

Russia saved the Jews
From total annihilation
at least in Europe.

That's how it happened,
        although Stalin never thought about it
And the people on the day of victory
        also never thought about it
And only a very few knew.

That's how it happened, but it could have been different.

Helmut, Hans, or Otto –
> One of the many
servants of the Führer
> but not with threatening weapons,
Nor in the medical unit, not with a scalpel,
> but with a movie camera – the eye
Taking in the destruction of life.

He recorded everything:
> tank movements, battles,
Russian prisoners
> trekking through the mud and pools,
Their doomed faces,
> and their eyes wandering off
To where the sun ends.

So on his film
> Their faces are fixed forever.
Their eyes survived.

And at the Last Judgement
> in his own defence he will present
This newsreel.

The Jonah Complex:
>   an escape from Soviet life
From the clutches of the KGB,
>   from the desire to take to the streets
And from the fear of arrest –
>   an escape into seas, oceans
Their unfathomable depth
>   submarine research
In the belly of a metal whale.

Borodino

Look here now, old man
        I built an uninhabitable
Mansion on the edge
        Of the field of Borodino, knowing nothing
except knowing
        there was a battle fought here once.
Well, some eggheads know about that,
        but for us an ostentatious house
Is a much bigger deal.

We could make a killing, though,
buying up this field
        with the bones of time gone by.
A place we could walk around in
        and set off fireworks
to commemorate a famous victory.

Then we could charge tourists admission,
And a fee for the show
        even build a hotel for them
On the hill
it would be terrific, old man.

A Russian Businessman on Patmos

Here we are in Patmos: a rocky cape, the sea,
A populated beach behind the grand hotel,
A waterfront café and a fresh morning breeze...
Unfulfilled, all those prophecies unfulfilled.

Back in Russia now, it's the Shadow holding sway.
And all the while you tremble, how bad it is for business.
Isn't it better like this, an extended holiday?
Here, seaside relaxation, and a life of laziness.

How pleasant just to sunbathe and inhale the healthy air
We don't believe in Judgement Day, we don't believe in God.
To hell with Russia... we could simply linger here
Carefree and on vacation, leave of absence without end.

Campaign Activity

An election for the arrival of spring!
Clear your eyes quickly,
                        Behold: ballot boxes
In a spacious, bright room
                        in the Temple of Elections.
Go there, they will hand you a green ballot
As green as foliage,
                        you'll drop it into the slot
Of the box garlanded with flowers,
                        right away the intoxication of April
Will hit you in the head,
                        and the day grow bright
And the birds sing,
                        and a drop start ringing.
But if you do not step up to that turquoise box
This will not happen,
                        Don't even hope.

Petromoscow. A new city
From the Nevà to the Moscow everything
Entangled in a net of streets, avenues,
                  choked to overflowing
With various automobiles
                  And myriads of eyes of
Cellular high-rises look out...

And the woods have vanished...
                  No trees, no birds, no wild animals
Except perhaps in reservations...

...*On the Last Wall*

They'll run the world without us,
                but we unexpectedly, in early morning
Will learn misery
                the collapse of a fragment of history.

The way a ship from Estonia
                in August 1940
Entered a distant port...
                The way its crew having gone off
Into the establishments of the port
                learn unexpectedly in early morning
That their homeland has vanished.

On an artificial island,
                    at the mouth of the Nevà River, you see a statue
With a gas torch
                    concrete-solid created
By order of the people,
            and given the name: 'Conscious
Necessity.'
            That means Liberty...
                        Not anarchy and savagery
Not robbery, not dissension,
                    But also not the one in New York City
That lifts its torch to the sky.

Pictures of the Future

1

Not with pen or brush
                    but with naked bodies on the square
Or in a green field
                    use them like calligraphy
Use them to write:
                    God is great.

Leave no witnesses
                    no witnesses...
Only God will see.

2

From Moscow to the Chukchi Sea
                    they have run the metro to the Bering Strait.
And now newlyweds
                    go there to look out
with a greedy eye – training binoculars
                    on Alaska and the far shore
(It may be snowy over there, but it's America.)

3

In the children's war
                    the call-up was called off
their parents are gone
                    lamented and forgotten...
Let's go to bed, lights out... Tomorrow morning at five
We'll rise – and off to war

In a far country

        to shoot down other children.
What can you do! Grown-ups got tired of fighting.

<h2 style="text-align:center">4</h2>

A painfully yellow spruce –

      yellow fir *
And you will not find any green...

      Evergreens are long gone
From our planet.

      There's just no green left.
The colour has been eliminated

      and while Earth has aged, children
In their non-green spring

      on mustardy grass in the yard
Play ball just the way they used to.

* These words are in English in the original text.

Souls, if they are immortal,
　　　　　after death, where exactly do they live?
In fragile memory, scrolling
Tapes of a completed life,
　　　　　films beyond all editing,
And sorrowing because
　　　　　there is no way to ask anyone
To retake the shot differently.

Tree on a hillside,
Tree under threads of rain,
In a sundrenched netting
a sea of rustling leaves.

Here it is – the tree of Life.

Notes to the Poems

HEROSTRATOS AND HEROSTRATOS (p. 27)

Herostratos burned down the temple of Diana at Ephesus, one of the Seven Wonders of the Ancient World, solely in order to achieve fame. The destruction worked: Who now remembers the names of those who built the beautiful temple?

'Black Stream': Черная речка, a landmark within present-day Leningrad, but once a stream-bank on the outskirts of St Petersburg, where Pushkin was fatally shot in a duel in 1837.

'Evgeny': the hero and victim of Pushkin's 'Bronze Horseman'.

'LOOK AT PAVKA CHICHIKOV...' (p. 53)
Pavel Ivanovich Chichikov: the protagonist of Gogol's *Dead Souls*.

JOB AND THE ARAB (p. 70)

'I, Job, I am that very Arab of the Qur'an': see 2:259 Surat Al-Baqarah (The Cow): 'Or [consider such an example] as the one who passed by a township which had fallen into ruin. He said, "How will Allah bring this to life after its death?" So Allah caused him to die for a hundred years; then He revived him. He said, "How long have you remained?" The man said, "I have remained a day or part of a day." He said, "Rather, you have remained one hundred years. Look at your food and your drink; it has not changed with time. And look at your donkey; and We will make you a sign for the people. And look at the bones [of this donkey] – how We raise them and then We cover them with flesh." And when it became clear to him, he said, "I know that Allah is over all things competent."'

ROBERT OPPENHEIMER AT THE FIRST TEST OF THE ATOM BOMB (p. 77)

The verses from the Bhagavad-Gita italicised in this English text are taken from a translation by George Thompson, North Point Press, 2008.

'O THE HOLOCAUST IN OŚWIĘCIM...' (p. 80)

The lines from Celan translate as, 'Your golden hair Margarete / Your ashen hair Shulamite'.

Oświęcim: the Polish name for Auschwitz.

BORODINO (p. 114)

The poem alludes not only to the devastating 1812 battle, but also to a poem written by Mikhail Lermontov (and translated by Alexander Hutchinson in *After Lermontov*, edited by Peter France, Carcanet 2014).

Acknowledgements

Some of these translations have been published in *Cyphers* (Ireland), *The Dirty Goat*, *Glas* (Russia), *Modern Poetry in Translation* (UK), *Naked Punch* (UK), *Poetry International*, *PN Review*, *The St Petersburg Review*, *Takahe* (New Zealand) as well as in the anthologies *In the Grip of Strange Thoughts* (Zephyr) and *Crossing Centuries* (Talisman).